The Moral Reform Union.

ELEVENTH ANNUAL REPORT:

AND

Account of Annual Meeting.

1892—1893.

To be obtained at the Office:

2, LEINSTER PLACE,
PORCHESTER TERRACE, LONDON, W.

PRICE SIX-PENCE.

The Moral Reform Union.

ESTABLISHED IN THE INTERESTS OF PURE FAMILY LIFE.

Office:

2, LEINSTER PLACE, PORCHESTER TERRACE, LONDON, W.

Office Hours, 2.30—5.30 *p.m.*

MOTTO:—"*Thou shalt love thy neighbour as thyself.*"—Matt. xix. 19.

OBJECTS.

I. To study, and confer upon, all subjects which especially affect the moral welfare of the young.

II. To collect, sell, distribute, or publish Literature for Moral Education.

III. To consider how best to carry out practical measures for the reform of public opinion, law, and custom on questions of sexual morality.

THIS Union will be in communication with Societies engaged in any branch of the work, such as—

The Social Purity Alliance.
The Societies for the Abolition of State Regulation of Vice.
The Society for the Suppression of the Traffic in Girls.
The Societies for the Protection of Young Servants.
Young Men's Christian Association.
The Peace and Arbitration Associations.
The Vigilance Associations.
The Personal Rights Association,
  and many others.

Reports and important papers of such Societies will be kept on hand.

No person eligible for *full* membership under the **age of twenty-five.**

The co-operation of members is invited for any branch of this work; and the business of the Union will continue to be conducted by those members who attend the meetings.

A Monthly Meeting is held at the Office on the first Wednesday of each month, and Ordinary Meetings on intermediate Wednesdays, at 3 p.m.

Drawing-room Meetings will be held occasionally, of which due notice will be given.

Subscriptions and Donations of any amount will be gladly received by

Mrs. MIERS, *Hon. Treasurer*, 74, Addison Road, Kensington, W.
Miss HELEN TAYLOR, *Hon. Secretary*, } 2, Leinster Place, W.
Miss F. E. ALBERT, *Secretary*, }

Bankers—THE NATIONAL BANK, 68, Gloucester Gardens, W.

" Unhasting,
   Unresting,
   Be each one fulfilling
His own God-given hest."—*Goëthe*.

MORAL REFORM UNION.

ELEVENTH ANNUAL REPORT,

1892-93.

OUR chief aim during the past year has been to foster the movement towards Moral Reform now manifesting itself with so much force. Fortuitous circumstances have enabled us to do this in some measure. For instance, in Germany, the activity of our Member, Frau Fischer-Lette, in writing and publishing, in promoting and attending Committees and Congresses on the Continent, has brought her into communication with the chief workers for Social Purity in that country, and has kept us informed of new movements there, which information we have passed on to the press ; an advantage to our German friends in England, leading them to apply for our publications. We have thus obtained the valuable co-operation at our weekly meetings of a German lady, when she is in England. But the principal cause for satisfaction with the progress of morality in Germany, is the appearance of Dr. Alfred Damm's remarkable book, "Die Krankheit der Welt" ; a work which probes fearlessly the deep world-canker, insisting before all things on personal purity and moral rectitude in the individual, if we would have a nation morally and, physically healthy. Dr. Damm gives new hope for future generations in his powerfully written monthly periodical, "*Die Wiedergeburt der Völker*" ("The Regeneration of the Nations"). Large book orders reached us from Vienna, so that this year we have touched Austria. By reciprocal intercourse we are endeavouring to help on the moral civilisation of nations now given over to Militarism.

American Congresses.—At the invitation of the American Branch of the International Council of Women, kindly transmitted by Lady Henry Somerset, President of the British Branch, we named Delegates to the Chicago International Congress of Representative Women, of May 15th to 22nd. Mrs. Miers was elected for the London Council, and it was specially hoped that Miss Taylor would represent the Union. This she kindly consented to do, and also drew up a Paper to be read on the occasion. Unfortunately, ill-health prevented her starting. But Frau Fischer-Lette, of Berlin, having, at Miss Taylor's request, been named Joint-Delegate, undertook the Mission, and remained for the World's Congress on Social Purity, of June 2nd-4th.

We desire to acknowledge our indebtedness to the Reception Committee for the courteous hospitality extended to our Delegate.

Mr. T. Anderson Hanson represented us at this latter Congress, consenting to read a Report condensing much of the Union's Work from its commencement, which we felt to be a useful survey. Both Delegates kindly undertook to distribute our literature.

We have in prospect the Convention of the World's Women's Christian Temperance Union, of October, which includes work for Social Purity. At this, Miss Conybeare will kindly be our representative.

Canada.—Our Member, Mr. D. A. Watt, of Montreal, continues his active efforts on behalf of minor girls. He was to contribute a Paper on "The Legal Status of Girlhood in Canada," to the Chicago World's Congress on Social Purity. We have passed on from him to the press, papers on various subjects. His co-operation is deeply valued by the Union.

New York.—"The National Christian League for the Promotion of Social Purity" has its head-quarters here. We have exchanged papers.

Sweden.—In response to a circular from Mrs. Butler, dated January, 1893, pointing out the danger of a measure proposed to be made law in Norway, Sweden, Finland, and Denmark, several Members of the Union and their friends, on February 14th, signed the Address to the Women of the Northern Countries of Europe, issued by the Ladies' National Association; and later on (March 11th) a special protest with 125 signatures was forwarded from the Moral Reform Union to Stockholm, to the Hon. M. Hugo Tamm, President of the British, General and Continental Federation, and was much appreciated by him. He stated that the names would be sent to Geneva.

France and Switzerland.—The Federation regularly transmits to us its papers and publications, which we gladly pass on to a French centre in London.

Belgium.—A Belgian gentleman, engaged in writing a voluminous work on social questions, made most careful enquiry at our office into our aims and working. Amongst other works he was presented with "A State Iniquity."

Cape Colony.—Since last year's Meeting, information received makes it evident that we must continue to leaven public opinion by means of our literature Miss Conybeare's speech at our last annual meeting has been widely distributed as a leaflet in the Colony.

Australia.—We have gladly strengthened the hands of our energetic member, Miss A. Bear, in her work for the Victorian Vigilance Association, by supplying her with literature for distribution. Another subject under our careful consideration relates to the Melbourne Women's Hospital.

India.—We rejoice that our Meeting at Exeter Hall, on January 12th, 1892, has been fruitful in results in India.*

The Union records its deep satisfaction at the election of its member, Mr. D. Naoroji, as the first Indian Parliamentary Representative, considering his success as a landmark in the moral growth of both England and India, and a promise of some measure of justice for the down-trodden women of the Indian races. "*The Indian Spectator,*" sent us weekly, is diligently studied, and gratifies us much by its encouragement of social reform in all its branches.

Memorial to Churches.—As early as July we approached the Decennial Indian Missionary Conference, and in October its Secretary notified us that a place had been made on the programme for a Session on Public Morals, before which the Memorial would be brought. A request was added for 300 copies, which we sent, with 100 of Mr. W. McLaren's speech in the House of Commons, and Mr. Maurice Gregory's speech at our last Annual Meeting in leaflet form. The unhappy result of certain business arrangements insisted on at that Conference by some persons, is known to all our friends. On the result becoming known to us, our last Report was sent to some missionaries on opposite sides—action perhaps more practical than merely recording our condemnation of a decision which all reformers must deplore.

Our Memorial has been sent to thirty-five important home centres, including the Church Congress at Folkestone, in addition to eighteen

---

* See "The Sentinel" for June, 1893, p. 67.

sent for the second time. It has also been sent to the Churches of Japan, the Chinese Christian Churches of Hong Kong and China, and the Churches of Liberia ; also to the Congress at Interlaken.

Literature.—1,147 works sold to March 31st, brought in £8 10s. 2d. —a slight increase over last year's business ; 2,438 works were distributed freely, to the value of £11 17s. 9d., and 268 works presented to us for distribution, and distributed, amounted to 17/9¾. We have to thank friends for many gifts of pamphlets and leaflets. Our literature has been freely distributed to friends in various countries— including Germany, Australia, Canada, the Cape, New Zealand, the United States, Newfoundland, Hayti, Bohemia, Roumania, Asia Minor, South America, India, Spain, Liberia, the Holy Land, and China.

A quantity of valuable old Repeal literature was presented to Mr. Aaron Powell, Chairman of the New York Committee for the Prevention of State Regulation of Vice and of the Chicago World's Social Purity Congress of June 2nd—4th. At the special request of one of our Church Members, some of our strongest Repeal literature was sent to Field Marshal Sir J. L. A. Simmons, who was to speak on the Church's Duty to Soldiers, at the Church Congress, Folkestone.

Our classified List of Works, as amended, was reprinted in April. It contains about 150 titles. It is a gratifying sign of the spread of morality, that it shows both French and German publications and Societies for Social Purity. Our thanks are due to friends who made special gifts for reprinting leaflets and for sending works to the Decennial I. M. Conference and to the Chicago Congresses.

Law Reform.—The pressing need of a stronger law to deal with crimes against morality in cases of near relationship, has been forced on the attention of our working members by the Assize Reports. We could wish earnest efforts made in this direction to strengthen the hands of the National Vigilance Association. Its Petition in support of the Amendments to the Criminal Law Amendment Act was signed by some of our Members.

We cannot forbear to express sympathy with the British Committee of the Federation in their earnest endeavours to unmask the Cantonment evils, and our rejoicing at the successful meeting of the Ladies' National Association of May 24th, when our friends from India, Mrs. Elizabeth Andrew and Dr. Kate Bushnell, made their statement of facts to the English public. Deeply impressed with the importance of their work, and the way it has been carried out in Africa as in India, we have invited these ladies to address us at our Eleventh Annual

Meeting. Our present Report will thus be the means of disseminating their valuable evidence in various quarters when next year's work calls us to distribute it as widely as that of last year.

Membership.—We desire to tender our hearty thanks to our Hon. Treasurer, Mrs. Miers; to express our deep sense of the constant and devoted services of our Chairman of weekly Meetings; and of the close interest and abundant generosity of our Honorary Secretary, Miss Taylor.

Obituary.—Death has robbed us this year of two of our most energetic Members. Both belonged to that earnest body, the Society of Friends. Miss Guglielma Stephens, of Bridport, last year moved the adoption of our Report. A constant attendant at the May Meetings, she ever urged social reforms on those she could influence. In this way she brought us this year the adhesion of two Members in the Orange Free State, and of an Editor in Tasmania. We shall miss her sympathy and co-operation.

Mr. Frederic Wheeler, of Rochester, was gathered to his reward on April 18th last, full of good works, at the great age of 85. He originated the agitation against flogging in the Army and Navy, worked hard in the Anti-Slavery cause, and, being domiciled in one of the "Protected Districts," became an uncompromising Repealer. He had an almost costless system of colportage for some years past, flooding the country round Rochester with Repeal literature, taking many occasions of spreading our papers. In every way his loss is to be deplored. His action in publishing and circulating facsimile copies of the appaling Bombay license for sin, set on foot the agitation now going on as to the Indian Cantonment Regulations. One of his last acts was a petition against the Opium Traffic.*

In spite of these losses, our numbers (175) exceed last year's by three, six members having joined; and the fact that one is an Icelander, and one a German lady, whilst three others are in widely scattered parts of the globe, shows that our work is extending its influence beyond the limits of England.

---

* Condensed from the Obituary Notice in *The Sentinel* for May, 1893.

MORAL REFORM UNION.

—

ANNUAL MEETING,
1893.

This Meeting took place on Wednesday, June 28th, at 74, Addison Road, London, W., by kind permission of Mrs. MIERS, the Hon. Treasurer; Mrs. CHARLES, Poor Law Guardian for Paddington, in the chair.

Mrs. CHARLES, in briefly opening the proceedings, referred to the work done by the Moral Reform Union as very thorough, and carried out with such persistency that the Society increased in value year by year. At the last Annual Meeting the subject of the break-down of Repeal in India was brought forward. Indeed the action taken by the Moral Reform Union had brought the matter before the whole world, for at the meeting held at Exeter Hall, on June 20th, the Rev. Hugh Price Hughes had said, with reference to the meeting held in the same place in January, 1892, under the auspices of this Society, that it had had the effect of stirring up the authorities at Lucknow to enforce the orders of the House of Commons. This was an evidence of the usefulness of this organisation. It was a matter of very deep regret that the Hon. Secretary, Miss Taylor, was not well enough to be present to-day; her generosity in helping forward every branch of work which came before the Society was beyond all praise. Very earnestly was it to be hoped she would very soon be able to be in England again.

Miss CONYBEARE moved the adoption of the Report and Financial Statement, which were taken as read. She was sure that the work of the Moral Reform Union had been of much benefit to the great Moral movement, and that gratitude was due to it for what it had accomplished. The Report showed that a great deal had been done to bring us into touch with moral reform in other countries. Special reference was made in it to Dr. Damm, who had given a great impetus to the movement in Germany. It was very satisfactory in the present crisis to have such a man as Mr. Naoroji on our side, and working with other Members of Parliament who were in sympathy with the movement against the State Regulation of Vice. Our interest ought to be very keen about what took place in other countries. We were too apt to be insular ; but we were the governing class in India, and were becoming the greatest power in Africa, and it was a great responsibility on our shoulders that we had introduced these laws into those countries. Our Government had it in its power to insist on these laws being swept away. Miss Conybeare had herself witnessed the contempt and loathing with which poor dark girls were regarded in Africa, and how they were treated worse than animals. The danger to English girls in going out there as servants was very great. The speaker had known two such cases ; one in which a girl was taken to a Lock Hospital and detained there without any proof against her but that of persons interested in upholding the system ; and of another who was similarly locked up for six months. The number of English girls in these places was, of course, small compared with Black girls, but there was no reason we should withhold our sympathy from the latter because they had dark skins. Personally Miss Conybeare was very grateful to the Moral Reform Union for having sent out such quantities of useful literature to Africa, and she hoped more would be forwarded. The conscience of England was now more awake than it had ever been before to these evils. We were realizing that ignorance was not innocence, and it was among our boys in the nursery that the moral training of our nation ought to begin.

Miss ABNEY WALKER seconded the Resolution. She remarked that the insiduous attempts in many places to revive or legalize State Regulation of Vice showed that this was no time to lay aside our moral armour, or relax vigilance, and certainly the Moral Reform Union would do neither whilst any danger remained. The recent action of the Decennial Indian Missionary Conference was a painful example of unfaithfulness to righteous convictions, for when called upon to denounce the deadly evils of Vice, Alcohol, and Opium, it practically endorsed them by its strange policy of silence. Social Purity workers might congratulate themselves on the election of Mr. Naoroji, and still more on having got a Departmental Committee appointed to enquire into the setting at naught of the order of the British Parliament of 1888. Lord Robert's denials had done harm in some quarters in tending to lull the public conscience. These C. D. Acts were very misleadingly termed by the blunted consciences of our State Officials and Army Surgeons "prudent measures for the protection of our soldiers' health," whereas their real root was the Devil's own lie that vice is a necessity. As to that unhappy class of Native women held in the most frightful form of "White Slavery," Lady Henry Somerset had said admirably :—" We pride ourselves on England having crushed out the flames of the Suttee, but this death was, in comparison, a chariot of fire carrying these poor women away from misery and degradation, compared to that *pit* of *horror* to which our English civilization has condemned them." We Moral Reformers put from us with horror the false and loathsome idea that the manhood of the nations would be undermined unless their womanhood be vilely sacrificed.

Dr. KATE BUSHNELL moved the following resolution :—

" That this Meeting hereby records its indignant protest against the outrages upon Indian women and the degradation of English lads and men, carried on in defiance of Parliament, under the East India Cantonments Act of 1889. And that this our protest be forwarded to the Right Honorable W.E. Gladstone and the Right Honorable the Earl of Kimberley, along with the expression of the determination of the majority of those here assembled in meeting to-day, to use all lawful means to unseat from power every man, without distinction of party, who continues to permit our country and its Queen to be disgraced by these iniquitous practices."

She said : " The resolution contains a reference to the East India Cantonments Act. There were what were called Cantonments Acts formerly, providing for exactly the same system as existed under the C. D. Acts. These Cantonment Acts were repealed after a resolution of the House of Commons forbidding the State Regulation of Vice in India. Therefore this second Act of 1889 was brought in. It provided for the establishment of hospitals, and gave very large, practically unlimited power to the Managers to detain any patients they thought proper. Mr. Stansfeld and Professor Stuart wrote a letter to Lord Cross quoting the resolution of the House which opposed the C. D. Acts in India, and which was passed on June 5th, 1888. In this letter to Lord Cross Mr. Stansfeld and Professor Stuart expressed what we know to have been a well-founded fear that the same system which existed under the C. D. Acts would be promulgated though not definitely set forth. In answer to the letter, Sir John E. Gorst, Under-Secretary for India, wrote on March 6th, 1890, stating that " the Secretary of State is unable to see anything in the rules which could lend any colour to the insinuations conveyed, and is unwilling to attribute to the Government of India an intention to evade the explicit instructions he has issued, unless some solid ground can be afforded for such an accusation." Now the British Committee were in possession of ground for this accusation, but to make assurance doubly sure, they requested

Mrs. Andrew and myself to pause, in our round-the-world trip for the Women's Christian Temperance Union, a sufficient time in India to make the necessary enquiry and investigation. We did so; we spent four months at the beginning of the year 1892 in investigation, sending home evidence immediately after; and we have since given evidence before the Departmental Committee. We are not here to-day to discuss the objectionable features of the C. D. Acts: in this we are all agreed; but to give you an opportunity of judging whether we are credible witnesses and can be trusted to give a fair and accurate report of the matters into which we inquired. I can affirm confidently that those regulations commonly known as the C. D. Acts are in operation still in the Military Cantonments of India. Now in this letter from Sir John Gorst to Mr. Stansfeld and Professor Stuart, he expressly states of certain " *Rules* " for the management of these Hospitals : "The Rules treat all persons alike who are suffering from contagious or infectious disorders," but in contradiction to that statement I hold in my hand a sentence, copied from a letter of instructions sent out from the Military Department of the Government of India to Cantonment Hospitals, Nov. 8th, 1892. This letter designates these same "Rules," and the instructions for the management of these hospitals is as follows : "The rules should be applied so as not to give legitimate cause of offence to respectable persons." There is no doubt at all as to which set of "Rules" Sir John Gorst refers to, and that it is the same set of Rules as this letter of instructions refers to, for the number and the section are quoted. But we all know that a hospital for women and for contagious diseases which is to be operated in such a manner as not to detain *respectable* women is a Lock Hospital. Formerly this particular class were called Cantonment Lock Hospitals, but the word " Lock " was taken out, and they are now simply called Cantonment Hospitals. This change of name conveys, and is intended, we have no doubt, to convey, an idea that the Hospitals are something different from former times : but the instruction I have just read shows they are in reality nothing but Lock Hospitals. During our sojourn in India we visited ten Cantonments. You all, no doubt, understand that a Cantonment in India is a section of country set aside for the residence of troops, and the law prevailing therein is a little different from that of the civil government of the country. In some cases no persons reside inside these Cantonments in any considerable numbers except the soldiers and the native tradesmen, but often there is likewise a large population of both British and native residents within them, who prefer this as being safer than outside : in different Cantonments the proportion of these varies greatly. The government inside these Cantonments is unlike that of the rest of India : it is a system of strict military law, and a person can be expelled without any reason being given. An instance occurred which showed us how this fear of expulsion might influence even the conduct of Englishmen. We were interested in the case of a girl, and secured the assistance of a gentleman to go into the magistrate's court, as we did not wish to go there ourselves, nor should we have understood the native language. At the close of the proceedings he told us what took place, and then he said "but you must promise me not to tell. I live within the Cantonment, and I could be sent out and no excuse given, so I cannot tell you these things unless you give me this promise." This showed what bonds that man felt himself under, and I speak of it that you may see that many of those who live within these Cantonments, and have property there, are placed in very embarrassing positions. I do not mean to offer any excuse for the silence of such persons, concerning what things are done, but I wish you to know that this Cantonment rule is like a rod of iron. But to return to my subject. We visited ten of the sixty or more Cantonments of British India. Now we have reason to conclude that to the *charges* we make no defence will come from India of the nature of an attempt to disprove what we have seen. It has indeed been admitted already in Indian newspapers we have seen that the spirit if not the letter of the law has been violated in *some* Cantonments. These are referred to as " exceptional cases." But from every one of the ten we went to we brought but one voice. Will the defence undertake to show that the ten Cantonments we went to were all exceptional, and none of those we happened to go to were governed in the ordinary way?

Let me read you some extracts from the Report of the Army Health Association for 1892 ; it is a most curious mixture of a plea for vice and for piety, the evil that is to be combated being " disease," not the breaking of the seventh commandment. This extraordinary document has been bound with a tract to put into the hands of the soldier lads called "Handbook for all Soldiers." Under the heading " How the chaplain can help men to escape disease," we read " Christ, the pure and holy Jesus 'Who gave Himself for us that He might redeem us from all iniquity' has said 'the things which are impossible with man are possible with God.' Try to keep from what leads to disease and ask God to help you, and you may be sure that you will get to be 'more than conquerors' over this evil." Blasphemous ! *Try* to keep from fornication, and God, through Jesus, will help you to overcome *disease !* It is no surprise then that under Section 2nd of this tract, "What the Medical Staff have to say," the soldiers are promised " Those who are infected will be kept as far as possible from coming in contact with you." Which, I take it, is a promise, in defiance of the House of Commons, that the C. D. Acts are and will be maintained in India. The further statement is made, "As long as any of you go in an underhand way out of bounds or take walks where you cannot be protected when you feel that temptation is on you, disease of the worst kind will prevail." Candid, to say the least ! and these young soldiers are to have placed in their hands what purports to be a religious tract in which assurance is given them that vice is made safe for them, and they must go openly, not secretly, but openly—like gentlemen, forsooth, to the " protected " places, " in bounds " when temptation is on them.

We are all familiar with the fact that, at the Decennial Missionary Conference, an attempt was made to move a resolution condemning the State Regulation of Vice, and I want you to see how the Major-General of the British Army, who wrote the introduction to the pamphlet I have quoted from, characterises that attempt :—

" At a Conference held in December in Bombay, the members of which had been drawn very much into the former anti-C. D. agitation, an attempt was made to hamper the Government of India in carrying out remedial measures at present practicable."

Thus for a Missionary Conference to condemn State Regulation of Vice is, on the word of a Major-General of India, to hamper the Government ! Will they go on calling upon us to prove our statements ? They have themselves put enough in our hands to prove the case. As I said, we visited ten Lock Hospitals, one in each of the ten Cantonments we went to. We found these " Lock Hospitals," by simply directing any cabman we hired at random, to drive us there. They always understood us. If they did not understand the English words " Lock Hospital" they always knew what was meant by the native term signifying " Hospital for disreputable women." And we can produce to-day the " Annual Report of the working of the Lock Hospitals for the North Western Provinces and for Oudh, printed at the Government Press of India, Allahabad, in 1890." It is thus by this name of Lock Hospitals that these Cantonment Hospitals are known in India, in spite of Sir John Gorst's statement that all patients are treated alike in them. I being a physician, we were allowed to see the records kept at these places, and we carefully examined the instruments, medicines, and the examination room, and made notes from the records kept. We saw the registration lists of the degraded women. We took care not to confuse the Registration Lists with the list of patients detained in Hospital. For instance, at Meerut we visited the Lock Hospital in February, and there were only five names' entered in the record of in-patients since the beginning of the year as detained in the hospitals, but in another book was a list of 100 women who were portioned off as belonging to certain regiments. The examinations were carried on by the British surgeon in the presence of the native surgeon and the nurse. We also saw at Meerut. in the Lock Hospital, records of complaints against certain women who were coming into the Cantonment for a pursuit of shame without permission, and in the hospital at Umballa we saw letters addressed by the British Surgeon to the Cantonment magistrate asking him to order up for inspection certain girls that had been pointed out by the soldiers as having been the cause of their illness. We also saw in the Lock Hospital at Meean Meer, orders for tickets addressed by the British Surgeon, to the Cantonment Magistrate, stating that so and so was enrolled to appear regularly at the bi-monthly examinations, and asking that a Registration Ticket be given her. From the dates on the remaining counterfoils, we proved that these orders had been used up to the time we visited the hospitals. One of the registration tickets corresponding to these orders will shortly be printed. We bought one from a degraded woman. On one side were stated her qualifications for sin—her age, &c.,—and the magistrate's name at the bottom; and on the reverse were dates which were initialled by the British Surgeon as noting that he had examined the condition of the girl. The last date was two days before we purchased the ticket. It will be curious to see how the authorities answer this. In one instance we tried to secure the release of a young woman from the brothel. I went to the magistrate's office to ask for the permit for a girl to leave the brothel, stating that she would be placed in a Mission Home. (Under the old system this " permit " was *openly* recognised as necessary : but even under the new regime the girl herself said she could not leave without one, and a native physician and several policemen said the same to me.) The magistrate replied that the permit was no longer required, but that it used to be long ago. Now, however, the girl was free to go any hour she wished. Then I said " These very policemen here in your court, told me the permit was still necessary." Then the magistrate replied, " these policemen do not know the law has changed." This will not do ; magistrates, who are British Military Officers, should be bound to see that their servants carry out the will of the House of Commons, and not their own will. However, we have the permit which the magistrate did issue to this young woman, and I saw him write it with his own hand. But we did not get her away on it ; she was one of the young, attractive girls, and in my presence the magistrate scolded and threatened her that if she once left the Cantonment it would be never to return. " But my mother is ill and dying ; she is in the Cantonment ; shall I never see her again ? " The magistrate declared she should never return, and moreover, that outside the Cantonment she should have no protection from the molestation of British soldiers. You can have no conception of the fear the native women have of the British soldiers. A Christian woman told me that a short time before she and her friends went into a village near Lucknow to preach the Gospel, but there was not a woman to be found in the place ; they had all hidden away ; they had suffered such shame and outrage from British soldiers who had passed through the village shortly before that they were frightened at the sight of a Christian. In consequence of this threat of insult and molestation from British soldiers and prohibition from ever seeing her mother again that girl is still in that Cantonment brothel, in that country which makes slaves of the women to preserve the health of the soldier. May God break these bonds !

Mrs. ELIZABETH ANDREW seconded the resolution. I have thought, she said, while Dr. Kate Bushnell was speaking of the Lock Hospitals, that it would perhaps be best if I were to show you the condition of the women in a somewhat different light. We visited twenty-two chaklas, seven in one Cantonment. It is difficult to describe the appearance of the women who dwell in these places. They do not wear a uniform dress ; their clothing is cheap and flimsy, and the chuddar which respectable women draw partly over the face these women wear thrown far back on their hair or even falling down on their shoulders. They often have a quantity of cheap jewellery, sometimes lent them by the Mahaldarni, to make them more attractive, or which they have bought from her and for which they are in debt. These women are frequently in debt to the Mahaldarnis. They told us, in many cases, that we were the first Christian women who had visited them. They said they knew that our God must be the true God because otherwise we should have been afraid to have come to them. In one chakla they said that a lady Missionary had been coming, but had discontinued her visits because she was informed she was injuring the Mission. In that chakla the Mahaldarni was exceedingly kind to the women. She had procured two Bibles since the visits of the Missionary, and was under deep conviction of sin. She said, " It is a wretched business ; I hate it all, but it is the only means I have of making a living by which I can keep myself out of sin. If I were to go out of the Cantonment, it would mean starvation." She begged us, if ever we could find a way to help them, to let her sister in Allahabad know also. She was a Mahaldarni too, and as anxious as herself to quit the life. Very cruel things have been said in the Press about Indian women. Assertions are constantly being made that these native women found in the chaklas are all brought up from the very beginning to an evil life, and that therefore no great harm is done them by forcing them into a degraded life. We wish totally to deny this. We inquired into the personal history of nearly 400 women. We found them to be of many nationalities and of all castes, and it was quite clear that the great proportion of these had not offered themselves, but had been brought into a life of shame. We found them suffering under a deep sense of shame at their degradation. When we questioned one as to the conditions in which we found them, often others would press round and say how they too loathed the life they were leading and the enforced examinations, and what tortures of shame they endured. One of the worst features of the system, to our thought, was the developement of brutality in the soldiers who frequently came to the chaklas drunken and riotous, and violently ill-used the women, who, as a Mahaldarni told us, fled in terror and tried to hide themselves; the Mahaldarni was powerless to protect them. A British surgeon in Agra told us that he wished to testify, after nineteen years' experience in India, to the morality of the native population, to their truthfulness and honesty; there was no such proportion of immorality as existed in England or America; the prostitute class was very small, and there were few Nautch girls and Temple women in proportion to the whole population. The Nautch girls, he said, could often command hundreds of rupees at a single wedding feast, when highly trained in voice and muscle. We visited them in their own quarters, in different cities; they considered themselves aristocrats in a life of degradation, and would scorn to go down to the level of "Government women," as the dwellers in the chaklas are called. The same surgeon to whom I have referred, said that there were very few prostitutes brought up to the life among the natives as a caste, or class, and there was no such immorality as that at home. A native physician, a graduate of Calcutta and professor in a medical college, also testified to the small number of the "prostitute class or caste." We received a letter, in answer to inquiries, from the Census Office, stating that the prostitute class was so small that no column had been left in the report for its enumeration, and yet that particular Cantonment was a perfect plague spot of the State Regulation of Vice.

A native gentleman, in Government employ for ten years, said to us that prostitution among the native women had greatly increased under British rule in India. Twice he said sadly, "*The Government does not care for the virtue of our women.*" We talked with the Mahaldarnis and the women under their charge, and we found everywhere, without exception, one sentiment of utter abhorrence and disgust, and a sense of shame and degradation with regard to the compulsory examinations. "Do the other women feel the same," we asked, when one of a group had given expression on different occasions to this sentiment, "Yes, we all hate them; not one is left out!" was the reply. Their feeling was unmistakable. Often they swayed to and fro, and beat their breasts, with tears running down their cheeks; they had the deepest feeling of their shame. They realised that it was not the

Queen, not the Home Government, by whom these things were done. They exclaimed more than once, " The Queen does not approve of these things ; she has ordered them to be stopped." " It is the Commander-in-Chief, the Colonel, and *your Christian men* who do these things," cried a woman on one occasion, and she stamped her foot, and flashed a look of reproach and misery upon us that I shall never forget. How was I to make her understand the difference between Christians and the men who could do these things ? They call the white men " Christians," and the black men " Natives." It was beyond her comprehension that those who were truly Christian would not tolerate these infamous Regulations, but she and the others understood our sympathy, and believed us when we said, " We are your sisters, and we are sorry for you." Then they would reply, " We are your slaves." Everywhere we learned that unless they obeyed the Regulations they would be expelled from the Cantonment. This meant starvation for them. We heard this on every hand, and a Missionary lady, who was many years in India, has corroborated that which we heard, that there are so few opportunities in that over-crowded country for women to earn a respectable living ; so few industrial openings of any sort for women : and as there is so little for respectable women to do you can see that work would not be given to those wretched degraded women, who have broken their caste by living with the soldiers, and so have become pariahs and outcasts. Then you must consider the immense difference which these poor creatures feel as existing between themselves and the conquering Anglo-Saxon race ; and they would not dare to complain against any injustice inflicted upon them. Yet even under these circumstances of enforced degradation we found the dignity of womanhood not utterly crushed out. To us, who have been through these experiences, these scenes are so real. We remember the expression of the women's faces, and the tone of their voices ; we had such a feeling for them that it seems to us unless God in His mercy had kept our hearts from breaking we could not have gone on seeing the scenes we did, and hearing the stories the women told us. One of the most terrible phases of this question is the brutalising of British lads. What lessons in vice and wickedness must they learn, and what contempt of womanhood will they not bring back to England ! We hear, indeed, from workers in this country of the tyranny in which vice holds these returned soldiers. What a prospect for the home-land ! What a future for the homes of England ! For it must come back to you, and the day will arrive when this sin and shame will be deeply felt in Great Britain. Not only, then, do we plead for the sake of our Indian sisters, but for the British youth sent out to India in such large numbers. We wish to call special attention to the Mahaldarnis. *We are convinced that they are notable figures in this tragedy which we witnessed. They are Government servants; in many cases they receive their salary from the Cantonment magistrate; they sometimes try to defend their position as respectable because they are employed by the Government. A Mahaldarni who introduced herself to us at Rawal Pindi, a very fine-looking, well-dressed woman, drew a book from her dress, showing her certificates as to service, these dating from April, 1887, to November, 1891, just three months before our visit. These letters and certificates recommended her for future services, and stated what she had done in the past; they were signed by British Colonels, Quartermasters, Surgeons, Chief Apothecaries, and others, with their full military titles appended. After this we saw such certificates in the hands of other Mahaldarnis. One, signed by the British Surgeon of a certain regiment, stated that she had furnished the regiment with prostitutes for three years, and recommended her to any other regiment needing her in a similar capacity. The Mahaldarni holding this shameful certificate declared to us that *she had been continuously in the service of the Government in that same Cantonment for ten years.* At our first visit to the chakla she was drawing ten rupees a month from the Cantonment magistrate. While visiting another Mahaldarni, I witnessed the purchase of her sixth girl. A well-dressed girl brought a wretched-looking girl in, and the Mahaldarni drew from the folds of her dress seven rupees and promised to pay eight annas more; this was a debt which the poor girl owed to the well-dressed one, they explained to me, and added "now the girl belongs to the Mahaldarni, who has paid her debt!" All present corroborated this to me. The degraded women are often in debt and very miserable. Another Mahaldarni with whom we talked, told us that when a new girl was needed in her chakla she went to the Cantonment magistrate and was furnished ten, twenty or fifty rupees; for a very young attractive girl, she said she was furnished fifty rupees. She added, "There is always plenty of money to get girls with." Thus is this shameful trade carried on. We saw three young girls in a chakla who had been brought in and registered for a life of shame, under fourteen years of age. We saw many very young girls in those dreadful places. When we think of them and of all the power brought to bear upon them, and of the slavery in which they live, and when we reflect that these cruelties are going on to-day just as they were a year ago, how can we give a sufficiency of prayer, of effort, of energy, and sympathy to have the whole system abolished! May God help us to answer the prayer of the Indian women, uttered as we were leaving them on several occasions, when lifting up their hands to Heaven, they asked God "to help us to help them."

The Resolution having been carried, a telegram was read from Mrs. Josephine Butler, regretting that at the last moment she was delayed from coming, as she had wished and intended to do. Mr. H. J. Wilson, M.P., telegraphed that he was detained in the House of Commons.

Miss F. ALBERT then stated that the Memorial from the Meeting, addressed to the Rt. Hon. W. E. Gladstone, M.P., the Rt. Hon. the Earl of Kimberley, the Rt. Hon. the Marquess of Ripon, the Rt. Hon. Ed. Marjoribanks, M.P., Secretary to the Treasury, and Geo. W. E. Russell, Esq., M.P., Under-Secretary for India, had only just arrived, there having been some delay in drafting it. The Memorial was as follows :—" That your Memorialists regard the existence of the State Regulation of Vice, in any form, as a violation of the Common Law, and consequently as a sentence of outlawry proclaimed against women ; and a denial of the Unity of the Moral Law and an encouragement to Vice. Your Memorialists hereby record their continued hostility to the system in any form, and renew the resolve to maintain constant vigilance against its re-introduction into Great Britain, to use every effort to obtain its entire abolition in India and the Crown Colonies, and further, as far as possible, to help the Abolitionist Movement on the Continent of Europe, and in our self-governing Colonies.

" Your Memorialists pray you to do your utmost to expedite the abolition of every form of this iniquity.
" Signed on benalf of the Meeting,
AMELIA CHARLES, *Chairman.*"

On the motion of Miss Conybeare, seconded by Dr. Bushnell, it was agreed that the Memorial should be sent in together with the Resolution.

Mrs. FISCHER-LETTE, Delegate from the M.R.U. to the Congress of Representative Women at Chicago, then read the following Address :—

Never, perhaps, in time of peace, has the Atlantic been crossed by such a large number of persons as during the present season. Weeks, nay months, before-hand every place was booked. Landing on Monday, May 1st, I went immediately to the office of the Guion line, but could not secure a berth before June 17th. I was, however, promised an earlier chance should any lady change her intention of starting.

I called upon Mr. Aaron Powell, the well-known President of the Social Purity Movement in North America, and he said to me in his courteous manner : " We should have been very sorry to miss you at the Social Purity Congress ; you must tell us about the German work."

Now as to the Women's Congress. The impression which everybody carried away was one of entire satisfaction. The members present numbered several hundreds, and they came from all parts of the globe. America opened wide her gates, and gave a cordial welcome to delegates from foreign lands. Not only was every nation of Europe well represented, but distant Asia and Australia had also sent delegates. All tongues were spoken, but, as was to be expected, English was the *Volapuk* of the day. Under such favourable conditions every one present could find some sympathetic soul, and some mind working on the same lines, and with the same aims as her own. The subjects under discussion were classed as follow :—

1. Education. 2. Industry. 3. Literature and Art. 4. Philanthropy and Charity. 5. Moral and Social Reform. 6. Religion. 7. Civil Law and Government. 8. Science and Philosophy.

The Meetings took place in the Art Building, situated in Adams Street and Michigan Avenue, in the morning between 10 and 1 o'clock, and in the evening from 8 till 10. Owing to the large number of Papers and Addresses sent in, from three to eleven rooms were occupied simultaneously. Over the entrance-door of each the title of the subject under discussion was plainly inscribed. One room was set apart for the reading, by their respective delegates, of the Reports of different societies, which were listened to with much attention. It was there that on Tuesday evening, May 16, I read the able Paper written by your Honorary Secretary, Miss Helen Taylor. There were about 200 present.

I might mention that the same evening Mrs. Ormiston Chant delivered an Address on her personal work in rescuing and giving shelter to erring men and women. Mrs. Beck Mejer, of Denmark, and other speakers followed. In the course of the evening a considerable number of those present—especially some of the American ladies to whom I had been introduced at the Reception on the previous day—questioned me with much interest about the work of your Society, and were very glad to take the literature you had sent for distribution. A suitable opportunity for making use of the remainder of the publications presented itself at some special early morning meetings, which were held daily from 9 to 10 a.m., and were attended by a few women who were working heart and soul for Moral Reform, and who gladly gathered together to discuss those laws and customs on which, in every country, vice and virtue more or less depend. To me these meetings were of the utmost value.

As nations mingle increasingly one with another, it becomes almost impossible to work exclusively within one's own country. It was, therefore, with deep regret I observed that not one of the other English delegates was present at these extra meetings. *Not one;* nor, indeed, a representative from any other country than America, except Madame Bertram, who works among theatre girls in London. Of course I told her of your efforts in that direction.

As the Northern States are a mixture of many nationalities, every European people has, it seems to me, its own especial duty towards this young and aspiring country. Yet we must beware of a Pharisaical attitude of superiority because of our long-established position ; we must, the rather, approach in a spirit of humility for our own short-comings, and with the consciousness that we have all done something to place stumbling-blocks in the path of the young giant. This was impressed upon me when I visited Refuges, Asylums, and Magdalene Homes in several of the cities.

As it was impossible to attend about eight meetings at the same time, we must wait for the Reports which the American Government has promised to print. Every day, during the Women's Congress, I sent a newspaper to Miss Taylor, and gladly communicated to her the expressions of high esteem and appreciation with which her name and that of your Society were received. On Monday, May 22nd, when Mrs. Potter Palmer once more threw open her palatial residence to receive us, Miss Susan B. Anthony, the well-known champion of every noble movement for the moral progress of womanhood, drew me to her side and presented to me the ladies who were pressing on to shake hands with her. As the representative of your Society, whose Hon. Secretary Miss Anthony holds in such high esteem, she called me her friend. From first to last there was but one sentiment of warm sympathy and friendly intercourse.

The next Congress is to take place in five years' time.

Meanwhile this Council of Women, and indeed every woman, should, in her own particular environment, do her best to maintain these cordial international relationships.

You may wonder that I have said nothing about the hospitalities that were lavished so profusely upon us foreign delegates. The receptions took place in the afternoon or late in the evening, and I must confess that with a view to keeping up strength and freshness for the business meetings I was obliged to forego the social attractions of the Congress.

Will you permit me to add a few words about the succeeding Congresses which I attended—the Medical, the Social Purity, and part of the Temperance Congress—all of which come into the domain of your Society. At all of them I ventured to describe myself as your delegate, and the name of your Society thus became widely known.

As a member of the British and Continental Federation, whose Conferences I have attended for more than ten years, I am well-known in that organisation, several of the Swiss representatives of which were present. Through speaking of the Social Purity Movement in Germany, now so well organised, I made many valuable acquaintances.

Another very honourable and agreeable charge was confided to me : Madame Isabelle Bogelot, the well-known President of the Work for Released Female Prisoners in France (prisoners from St. Lazare), asked me to speak of the work of her Society, because, she gracefully put it, " You are a German." I was prevented, by some accident from reading the paper I had prepared. I wrote to Madame Bogelot about it, and found, on arriving here, a most kind and courteous letter giving me full permission to write about her work in the English and German newspapers.

By the kind help of the highly respected sisters, Dr. Elizabeth Blackwell (of England) and Dr. Emily Blackwell (of New York), I received valuable introductions and permission to visit institutions of Moral Reform in America.

In conclusion I wish to say that I am fully conscious of your confidence, and shall more than ever endeavour to promote the noble objects of your Society—objects which are at one with the motto on which I work :—" Do ye not know that your body is the temple of God, and that the Spirit of God dwelleth in you ? "

On the motion of the Chairman, seconded by Miss F. Albert, and supported by Dr. E. Blackwell, a vote of thanks was passed to Mrs. Fischer-Lette.

Miss LORD moved a vote of thanks to Mrs. Miers for her kindness in having the meeting held at her house. She said that it was just two years since they had met under that same hospitable roof to listen to the two American ladies who had just been speaking, but on that occasion it was with reference chiefly to work in their own country. The work was world-wide, for no country was perfect or could set itself up as a model to other countries. It was with the greatest pleasure that she proposed a vote of thanks to Mrs. Miers who was so heartily in sympathy with the work of the Moral Reform Union and laboured unremittingly for its objects.

Miss EMILY HILL seconded, referring to the warm feeling of esteem entertained for Mrs. Miers by her fellow-workers.

The Rev. HENRY SOLLY moved a vote of thanks to the Chairman. He said he much wished that several persons who did not understand this serious and solemn question they had been discussing, had been present to have been enlightened. One lady, who had been in India, told him that she thought there was so much on both sides she did

not dare face the subject.   If she could have been present she would
have realised that there could not be two sides to such a question.
The speaker went on to emphasize the necessity of manly chastity,
and pointed out that there was now less excuse for wrong-doing on
the part of soldiers, inasmuch as the times of service were shorter.
Even as far back as the days of Cæsar chastity was held up as a chief
masculine virtue.   In Cæsar's armies that man was held in the highest
honour who led the most chaste life.   The reverend gentleman trusted
that pressure would be brought to bear on the Government authorities
to induce them to take a manlier view of the question and an end be put
to the present iniquity.   He was very thankful that such a society as
the M.R.U. was in existence, and he thought its claims had been too
little brought before the public.   He hoped it would receive that
larger support which it deserved, though, considering the number of
societies, he felt that something should be devised to economize the
strength, moral and religious, as well as pecuniary, of the workers.

Miss GOFF seconded the vote, and spoke of the salutary change
which had been effected by the work of the Union.

Miss F. ALBERT, in putting the motion, said a sympathetic letter
had been received from Paris, from Mdlle. Wyld, a member.

The Chairman having acknowledged the vote, the meeting
concluded.

SUBSCRIPTIONS AND DONATIONS.

	Subs. £ s. d.	Dons. £ s. d.
Atkey, Mrs.	1 1 0	
A. D. A.	0 5 0	
A Friend		1 0 0
Albert, Miss F. E. (Secretary)	0 2 6	
Browne, Mrs. Woolcott (Founder)	25 0 0	
Browne, Miss	1 1 0	
Blackwell, Dr. Elizabeth	0 5 0	
Barham, Miss Foster	1 0 0	
Bird, Miss	0 5 0	
Burd, A. A., Esq. (*Ireland*)	0 5 0	
Buss, Mrs. Septimus	0 2 6	
Buckle, Miss	0 2 6	
Bussell, Miss Ada G.	0 2 6	
Brodribb, Miss F.	0 2 6	
Bennett, Miss E.	1 1 0	
Blacker, Mrs. Louis (*Germany*)	1 0 0	
Burt, C. W., Esq.	1 1 0	
Burt, Mrs. C. Johnstone	0 5 0	
Brandreth, H. S., Esq.	1 0 0	
Charles, Mrs., P.L.G.	0 10 0	
Cobb, Mrs. H. P.	0 5 0	
Collet, Miss S. D.	0 2 6	
Cock, Mrs. Astley	0 5 0	
Carslake, Mrs. Hawkey	1 1 0	
Coles, Mrs.		0 10 6
Conybeare, Miss	0 2 6	
Dobson, Rev. T. R.	0 10 6	
Evans, Mrs.	0 4 0	
Eccles, Mr. and Mrs. A. E.	2 2 0	
Estlin, Miss	0 10 6	
Ford, Mrs. Rawlinson	0 2 6	
Ford, Miss I. O.	0 10 0	
Goff, Miss A.	0 5 0	
Geddes, Rev. J. C. B. and Mrs. Geddes (*Scotland*)	0 12 6	
Hall, Miss	0 2 6	
Hanson, T. Anderson, Esq.	0 10 0	
Heath, Mrs.	0 3 0	
Hill, Miss Emily	0 5 0	
Hill, Miss Sarah	0 5 0	
Hindley, Mrs.	0 10 0	
Hunter, Mrs. Stephenson	1 1 0	
Hodgson, Mrs. (*Scotland*)	0 2 6	
Horsley, H., Esq.	0 5 0	
Johnson, Miss Agnes	0 2 6	
Jones, Rev. E. Ceredig	0 2 6	
J. S. M.	0 2 6	
James, Mr. and Mrs. Thomas (*Orange Free States*)	0 10 0	

	Subs. £ s. d.	Dons. £ s. d.
A. K.	0 10 0	
Leach, Mrs.	0 5 0	
Lord, Miss F.	0 2 6	
Mills, Halford L., Esq.	1 1 0	
Miers, Mrs.	1 0 0	
Mitchell, Mrs. C. T.	0 10 0	
Mitcheson, Mrs. T.	0 2 6	
Munroe, Mrs.	0 2 6	
Mason, Miss C.	0 10 0	
Mordan, Miss C. E.	0 2 6	
Malleson, W. T., Esq.	0 2 6	
Meredith, Rev. W. M.	0 5 0	
McNaughten, Mrs.		0 2 6
Müller, Mrs.	1 1 0	
Martineau, The Rev. James, D.D.		1 1 0
Newman, Professor F. W.	2 0 0	
Newcombe, Mrs. S. Prout	1 0 0	
Naoroji, D. G., Esq.	0 10 6	
Owen, Rev. G. A.		0 5 0
Prior, Miss A. A.		0 2 0
Parnell, Miss Mary	0 5 0	
Phillips, Mrs. W.	0 5 0	
Pallandt, Baroness de	0 5 0	
Peppercorn, Miss A. E.	0 5 0	
Paggi, Madame		0 10 0
Peacock, Mrs.		0 2 6
Payne, Mrs.	0 5 0	
Reed, Mrs. E.	0 5 0	
Southey, Mrs.	0 5 0	
Stivens, Mrs.	0 5 0	
Stammwitz, Miss L.	0 5 0	
Smith, Rev. A.	0 2 6	
Shuttleworth, Miss K.	1 1 0	
Swanwick, Miss	1 1 0	
Smith, Mrs. Pearsall	0 5 0	
Strickland, Mrs. F.	0 4 0	
Stansfeld, Rt. Hon. James, M.P., and Mrs.	0 5 0	
Sherrard, J., Esq., J.P.	0 2 6	
Solly, Rev. H.	0 2 6	
Thomas, Mrs. E.	0 10 0	
Thomas, Mrs. C.	1 0 0	
Turner, Mrs.	0 5 0	
Tremenheere, Mrs.	1 1 0	
Taylor, Miss Helen (Hon. Sec.), special donation		17 10 0
Tebb, Mrs. W.	1 1 0	
Tubbs, Mrs.	0 10 6	
Tolme, Mrs.	1 1 0	
Toller, Mrs.	1 1 0	
Tucker, Mrs.	0 10 0	
Thompson, Mr. and Mrs. F.	0 10 0	
Walker, Miss Abney	0 5 0	
Wells, Mrs. T. H.	0 5 0	
Weymouth, Miss	0 2 6	
Whale, Mrs.	0 5 0	
Wheeler, F., Esq., the late	1 1 0	
Williams, Alf., Esq. (2 years)	0 5 0	

					Subs. £ s. d.	Dons. £ s. d.
Williams, Mrs. Wilfrid	..	..	..	..	0 5 0	
Weiss, Mrs. C.	..	..	..	..	0 5 0	
Whitehead, Miss, 1892—3	..	..	..	..	0 10 0	
Wates, Joseph, Esq.	..	..	..	..	1 1 0	
Wilkinson, Miss	..	..	..	..	0 5 0	
Wilson, H. J., Esq., M.P.	..	..	..	..	0 10 0	
Wilson, Mrs. H. J.	..	..	..	..	0 10 0	
Watt, D. A., Esq. (Montreal)	..	..	..	..	0 10 0	
Weppner, Fräulein (Germany)	..	..	..			0 10 0

The following are also Members :—

Ashford, Mrs., P.L.G.
Askey, Mr. and Mrs. F.
Balgarnie, Miss F.
Banks, F. C., Esq.
Barbosa, Mrs. Garnett (Liberia)
Bazett, Rev. H.
Bear, Miss A. (Australia)
Berdoe, Edward, Esq., M.D.
Bradley, Mrs.
Bullen, The Rev. R. A., M.A.
Burnett, Miss Mary
Chant, Mrs. Ormiston
Chapman, Miss E. R.
Clifford, Rev. John, D.D., LL.B.
Clifford, Mrs.
Campbell, Mrs.
Clelland, Mme.
Cozens, Miss
Drew, Mrs.
Dymond, Mrs. George
Fischer-Lette Frau (Germany)
Gilder, Mr. Dhanjibhai Dorabji (India)
Hack, Mrs. Brocklehurst
Haines, Mrs.
Hammond, Eric, Esq.
Herbert, Jesse, Esq., Barr.
Hime, C. Maurice, Esq., M.A., LL.D.
Hoggan, Mrs. Frances, M.D. (Continent)
Hessë, Mr. Emil (Sweden)
Keer, Mrs. Clarke
Kilgour, Miss
Knight, A. A., Esq.
Kidd, Mrs.
Kirby, The Rev. J. C. (Australia)
Law, Mrs.

Löfving, Miss Concordia (Sweden)
Lodge, L., Esq. (Tasmania)
McLaren, John Shaw, Esq., M.D.
Magnüsson, Mrs.
Meredith, Mrs.
Minet, Miss G. (Australia)
Misra, U. S., Esq., B.U.C.S. (India)
Mitcheson, The Rev. T.
Moore, Mrs. R.
Müller, Miss
Nathan, Mrs. H.
Newcombe, S. Prout, Esq.
Ockenden, James, Esq.
Pease, T. H. O., Esq.
Rossell-Jones, Mrs.
Rudge, Miss
Sherrard, Mrs.
Steinthal, The Rev. A. S.
Steward, Mrs. (of Ongar)
Storr, F., Esq.
Streatfeild, Mr. and Mrs. W. H.
Teschmacher, Mrs.
Thomas, Miss R.
Timmins, Rev. T.
Tod, Miss Isabella (Ireland)
Trepplin, Mrs.
Toùrnier, Miss
Varley, Mrs. Henry (Australia)
Venning, Miss
Walters, Mrs.
Williams, Rev. Henry
Williams, Mrs. Howard
Williams, Miss Jane
Wild, Mdlle. (Angèle de St. Françoise), (France)

THE MORAL REFORM UNION.

Statement of Accounts from 1st April, 1892, to 31st March, 1893.

Receipts.

	£ s. d.	£ s. d.
To Balance in hand, 1st April, 1892—		
Bank ...	48 14 0	
Cash ...	13 12 1	62 6 1
„ Subscriptions and Donations ...		56 8 10
„ Special Donations—		
Mrs. Woolcott Brown	25 0 0	
Miss Helen Taylor ...	27 10 0	52 10 0
„ Sale of Literature ...		13 9 7
		£184 14 6

Expenditure.

	£ s. d.	£ s. d.
By Rent of Office ...		35 0 0
„ Literature ...		8 10 2
„ Stationery and Sundries ...		1 18 5
„ Secretary's Salary ...		70 0 0
„ Printing ...		11 6 6
„ Postage ...		8 2 2
„ Firing, Lighting, Office Expenses, and Caretaker ...		17 12 6
„ Audit Fee ...		1 11 6
		£154 1 3
„ Balance at Bank ...	25 19 8	
Cash in hand ...	4 13 7	30 13 3
		£184 14 6

Examined, compared with the Books and Vouchers, and found correct,

M. HARRIS SMITH, *Auditor.*
(PUBLIC ACCOUNTANT.)

13, Victoria Street, Westminster, S.W., and
Royal Bank Buildings,
123, Bishopsgate Street Within, E.C.

10th April, 1893.

—

BURT & SONS,
Printers and Publishers,
58, Porchester Road,
Bayswater, W.

—

www.ingramcontent.com/pod-product-compliance
Lightning Source LLC
Chambersburg PA
CBHW081308040426

42452CB00014B/2704